MW01098120

San Antonio's Historic Plazas, Parks and River Walk

in Vintage Postcard Images

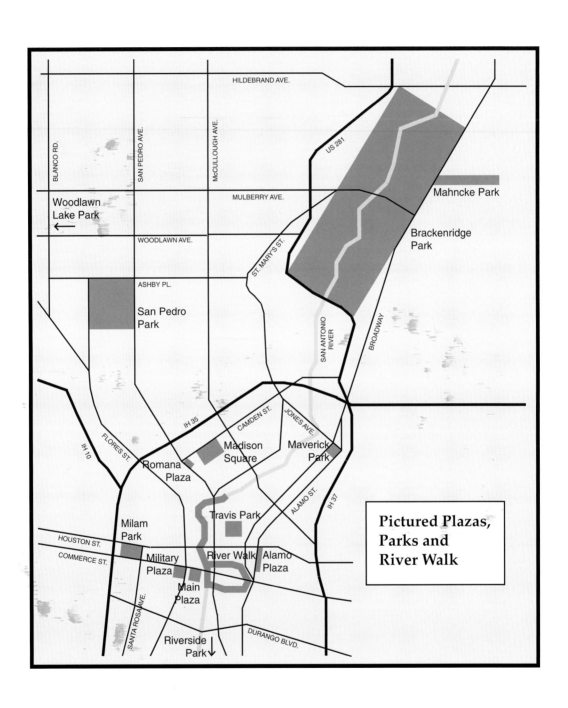

HILDEBRAND AVE.

BLANCO RD.

SAN PEDRO AVE.

McCULLOUGH AVE.

US 281

Mahncke Park

MULBERRY AVE.

Woodlawn
Lake Park
←

WOODLAWN AVE.

ST. MARY'S ST.

Brackenridge
Park

ASHBY PL.

San Pedro
Park

SAN ANTONIO RIVER

BROADWAY

IH 35

CAMDEN ST.

JONES AVE.

IH 10

FLORES ST.

Madison
Square

Maverick
Park

Romana
Plaza

ALAMO ST.

IH 37

Travis Park

Milam
Park

HOUSTON ST.

COMMERCE ST.

Military
Plaza

River Walk

Alamo
Plaza

Main
Plaza

SANTA ROSA AVE.

Riverside
Park ↓

DURANGO BLVD.

**Pictured Plazas,
Parks and
River Walk**

San Antonio's Historic Plazas, Parks and River Walk

in Vintage Postcard Images

Lewis F. Fisher

Maverick Publishing Company

MAVERICK PUBLISHING COMPANY
P.O. Box 6355, San Antonio, Texas 78209

OTHER BOOKS OF VINTAGE POSTCARD IMAGES
Eyes Right! A Vintage Postcard Profile of San Antonio's Military by Lewis F. Fisher
Alamo to Espada: A Vintage Postcard Profile of San Antonio's Spanish Missions by Lewis F. Fisher

Library of Congress Cataloging-in-Publication Data

Fisher, Lewis F.
     San Antonio's historic plazas, parks and river walk : in vintage postcard
images / Lewis F. Fisher
          p. cm.
Includes index.
     ISBN 1-893271-27-7
  1. Plazas–Texas–San Antonio–Pictorial works. 2. Parks–Texas–San Antonio–
Pictorial works. 3. Historic sites–Texas–San Antonio–Pictorial works. 4. Pasel del
Rio (San Antonio, Tex.)–Pictorial works. 5. San Antonio (Tex.)–History–20th century–
Pictorial works. 6. Postcards–Texas–San Antonio. I. Title.
     F394.S2117 A24 2002
     976.4'351'00222–dc21
                                                                                    2002151796

5 4 3 2 1

Printed in the United States of America

ABBREVIATIONS IN CAPTIONS: Postcard publishers' names, when
known, appear in italics at the end of each description. "n.p." stands
for no publisher identified, "pm." for postmarked. In the absence
of a postmark, the publication date is estimated.

Contents

San Antonio River from Mill Bridge. San Antonio, Tex.

Brush was being trimmed along the San Antonio River downtown—the first step in the evolution of the River Walk—when this view was taken toward the courthouse. *(George M. Bearce, San Antonio, pm. 1909)*

Foreword: Urban Windows

Twenty-first-century San Antonians live within two landscapes, one more noticeable than the other. The older, less distinct one shapes the central business district and such nearby residential areas as King William. These were designed for walking. As we stroll their sidewalks and their open spaces, we directly interact with our fellow citizens and the surrounding urban fabric.

The other, much more dominant environment, is structured to meet the needs of mechanized transport, from early streetcars to late-model SUVs. Over the past century, these ever- faster forms of transportation have transformed the city center and its widening periphery. Today, far from the downtown core, exists an expansive, car-driven sprawl of high-speed freeways, mega malls and gated subdivisions, each segregated from the other, accessible only by four wheels.

To recover a sense of that older, pedestrian cityscape one need but leaf through this lovely collection of images depicting San Antonio's historic plazas and parks, and the river that meanders through them. These postcards wonderfully evoke San Antonio before the needs of the car—and its drivers—determined development patterns.

They also remind us how important these spaces were in shaping how people met in public and in framing visitors' experiences of this bustling metropolis. Even the political leadership recognized that urban parks were an integral expression of the city. In 1950 Stewart King, then superintendent of parks, said that the number of plazas and parks was largely responsible for San Antonio's "distinctive charm"and the frequent comment, "There are only three interesting cities in the United States—San Francisco, New Orleans and San Antonio."

The connection King made between parks and charm has been replicated in most nineteenth- and early-twentieth-century guidebooks. As bookseller and postcard publisher Nic Tengg's 1908 guide asserted: San Antonio has "often [been] called the City of Parks on account of the many ornamental parks and plazas with which it is adorned."

That this sort of open landscape left a memorable impression was precisely what eighteenth-century Spanish urban planners had in mind when they designed San Antonio and other cities within their vast New World empire. Framed around a grid that led citizens of this frontier town to revolve around San Fernando Cathedral for all daily activities, this circulation pattern reinforced the church's role as civic hub and created a vibrant street life. Main and Military plazas, which opened to the east and west of the cathedral, became centers of commercial trade and social exchange, and functioned as the communal heart.

Other open spaces, such as Alamo Plaza and Milam Park, served similar needs.

The pattern was reproduced in the next century with the creation of Maverick Park and Madison, Washington, and Franklin squares. Each offered the face-to-face interactions that earlier planners deemed so necessary to a healthy civic life. As revealed in this book's vintage views of crowded sidewalks and swimming holes, San Antonians took full advantage of their many opportunities to mingle in The Great Outdoors.

The notion of shared civic space slowly disappeared with the railroad's arrival in 1877. The city's commercial orientation re-centered around the railroad terminals directly to the east and west of downtown. Streets in between were widened to facilitate cross-town movement of bulky cargo. Streetcar lines were laid down to haul passengers from one rail line to the other, and also carried residents to new suburbs radiating from the central core.

As population expanded, once-open plazas were filled in. A new city hall swallowed up Military Plaza. Main Plaza lost ground to widened streets, as did Alamo Plaza. Others were sliced in two by streets supposed to speed up traffic flow. This "whirl of modern life," novelist Stephen Crane wrote in 1889 after visiting the Alamo City, destroyed San Antonio's fabled past, trampling it into "shapeless dust." The greatest culprit, he mused, was the "almighty trolley car."

The automobile only added to these emerging complications. Even as cars provided access to a broader range of experiences and landscapes, they rearranged the context in which we encountered one another and the built environment. Note the number of vehicles parked around Main Plaza (page 9) and bunched up along Alamo Plaza (page 19), a visual disarray that signaled serious traffic congestion downtown. Similar bottlenecks would disrupt the experience of the many who traveled to Brackenridge Park and the zoo and who required an increasingly larger number of dedicated parking spots. This growing, city-wide consumption of space—to say nothing of accelerated frustrations associated with trying to find parking—continues to shape the modern temper.

So where does the early-twentieth-first century citizen go for a brief respite from the spinning demands of our fast-paced life? To the same landscape to which San Antonians have always flocked—the river. We may no longer draw our potable water directly from its flow, bathe in it or roll our carriages across its gravelly fords, but we still esteem it as the key feature of our environment. Like preceding generations, we wander its banks, float down its placid waters and jostle one another for a better view of passing parades. Like them, we are there to see and be seen, to participate in the colorful and pulsating urban spectacle.

That's why open space is so critical, the *San Antonio Express-News* argued in 1919: "A city without parks is like a house without windows."

Char Miller
History Department, Trinity University

Introduction

When picture postcards burstonto the scene a century ago, they provided a bonanza for those seeking clues to the evolution of the present era.

As the largest city in Texas from 1890 to 1930—the height of postcards' greatest popularity—San Antonio was a target market for postcard sales, to the growing number of residents as well as to waves of tourists visiting the picturesque place. As a result, San Antonio's rapidly-changing scene was particularly well documented, including the evolution of its public spaces.

Postcards came onto the scene rather quickly. At the end of the 19th century photography was widespread, but not yet accessible to everyone; nor could newspaper presses yet publish photographic illustrations with clarity. But German printers had perfected the manufacture of photographs as lithographs on high-quality cards. Soon Europeans were buying and mailing views of their hometowns and vacation spots to friends and relatives everywhere.

In 1898 the U.S. Post Office Department caught up with its overseas counterparts. It allowed low postal rates for privately printed cards of specific dimensions as long as there was nothing but the address on one side; personal notes had to be written on the same side as the illustration. Then authorities relented and let messages be written in a designated area on the back, so illustrations could occupy the entire front side.

With mailing inexpensive, postcard manufacturing became big business. Americans seized upon them not only to share familiar scenes with others but also to send brief messages—even just across town, for telephones were not yet widely used and were often undependable, and long distance calls were expensive if they could be made at all.

In 1902, as new cameras could accommodate film in small rolls, manufacturers came up with cardstock photographic paper with preprinted backs. Custom-made photos could now be mailed as postcards. In 1908, the Post Office Department reported that 667 million postcards of all types had gone through the mail that year. Five years later the total was above 968 million, fueled by a collecting exchange craze that brought one postcard club—in Philadelphia—10,000 members.

The bubble began to burst when postcards' greeting function was challenged by folded cards mailed in envelopes, as better telephones came out and when World War I cut off access to German printers, though postcards remained popular and still document the passing scene.

The 166 postcard images in this book—from collections of the late Ilse Griffith and others—uniquely illuminate development of San Antonio's plazas, parks and River Walk. All of the city's major historic parks are represented as well as a number of lesser ones. Images of some smaller, less developed early parks could not be found, including two 1870s parks in the vicinity of Milam Park—Franklin Square, now Columbus Park, to the north, and, to the south, now-vanished Washington Square; Crockett Park (1875), northwest of Madison Park; Dawson Park (1890) in the East End development; Rosedale Park (1892) at Elmendorf Lake; King William Park (1901) near downtown; and, in southern San Antonio, Palm Heights Park (1910) and Collins Gardens Park (1917).

I am grateful to Dr. Char Miller, chairman of Trinity University's history department, for providing historical context in a foreword, and, for many of the details, to *San Antonio Express-News* history columnist Paula Allen and to Maria Watson Pfeiffer, former special projects officer for San Antonio's Parks and Recreation Department.

1. Military Plaza

The handful of Spanish soldiers who came with the founders of San Antonio in 1718 moved four years later from their garrison near San Pedro Springs to a presidio on the newly located Military Plaza, or Plaza de las Armas. At its northwest corner the presidio commander's home still bears the date 1749, and is now known as the Spanish Governor's Palace.

San Antonio became the region's transportation center. Military Plaza was its hub, with stagecoaches and wagons of all types gathering there and departing for various points on the frontier. By 1877, however, the cries of teamsters and chile vendors—the fast-food merchants of the day—began to dwindle on Military Plaza with arrival of the railroad, as the distribution hub shifted to the new train station a mile to the east.

In 1891, a new city hall was built in the center of the nearly-deserted plaza. There, renovated, it remains, with those surrounding buildings that once served stagecoaches and wagon trains now converted to office or other retail use.

Still in the heart of a spreading city, San Fernando Cathedral, in center foreground, faces Main Plaza. Behind it, City Hall stands in the center of the once open Military Plaza. (*Charles Lemic Photocard, Pittsburgh, 1949*)

Commercial buildings enclose Military Plaza and City Hall, its centerpiece since 1891. *(Nic Tengg, San Antonio, ca. 1915)*

City Hall. San Antonio, Texas.

Ed. Sachs, Pub. San Antonio, Tex.

San Antonio's ornate Second Empire-style City Hall was crowned in its center by a 135-foot octagonal tower and cupola topped by the city clock. *(Ed Sachs, San Antonio, ca. 1905)*

Seen from its northwest corner looking southeast, beyond City Hall and facing Main Plaza are the spires of San Fernando cathedral, left, and Bexar County Courthouse. *(n.p., ca. 1910)*

Built in the mid-18th century for the presidio commander and now known as the Governor's Palace, this is the only Spanish residence of its type surviving in Texas. *(n.p., ca. 1935)*

After the Spanish Governor's Palace restoration in 1931, this reception room and other areas were furnished with antiques of the period. *(n.p., ca. 1935)*

INTERIOR—GOVERNOR'S PALACE, SAN ANTONIO, TEXAS

The caption on the back of this card explains that the troubadour inside the courtyard is "serenading his sweetheart, an old Spanish custom." *(Nic Tengg, San Antonio, ca. 1935)*

Pebbles laid in concrete pave the romantic courtyard of
the restored Governor's Palace. *(n.p., ca. 1935)*

Mexican Candy Vender,
on Military Plaza,
San Antonio, Texas.

These candy sellers are holdovers from the time of itinerant vendors who thronged Military Plaza when it was a transportation center. *(Dahrooge Post Card Co., San Antonio, pm. 1912)*

2. Main Plaza

San Antonio's largest immigrant group in Spanish colonial times—more than 50 settlers from the Canary Islands—arrived in 1731 and set up the Villa de San Fernando de Bexar on the new Main Plaza, or Plaza de las Islas. The plaza was soon dominated on its west by the new church, its original apse left in place when construction began in 1868 on the new walls and twin towers.

Across from the church stood the Casa Reales, meeting place for the town council, its site eliminated in the 1920s with construction of a San Antonio River flood control channel. The channel has since been integrated with the River Walk and linked with Main Plaza through a new park at the plaza's northeast corner.

Main Plaza's original function as center of the civilian community remains, not only with the religious function with the venerable cathedral but also the governmental function. Main Plaza is home to both the Bexar County Courthouse and, once again, the city council, its chambers now on the ground floor of the 1921 bank building beside the cathedral.

Main Plaza Looking South. Court House on the left. San Fernando Cathedral on the right. San Antonio, Texas.

Construction of a courthouse on the south side of Main Plaza in 1892 gave San Fernando Cathedral a companion landmark. *(Adolph Selige Pub. Co., St. Louis, pm. 1908)*

Narrow streets opening onto a broad plaza are evident in this view from the courthouse to the northwest. *(International Post Card Co., New York, ca. 1905)*

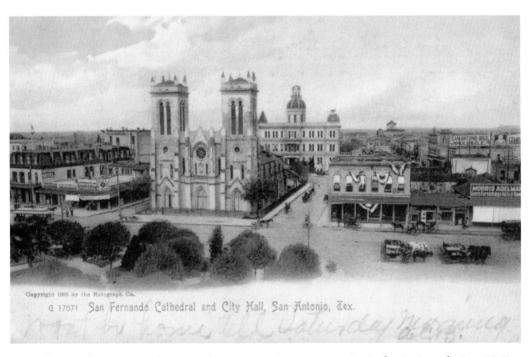

Here the Southern Hotel shows at the far left of San Fernando Cathedral, with City Hall and Military Plaza behind it. At its right is the two-story Frost National Bank and beyond it Morris Adelman's hat and shoe store. *(Rotograph Co., New York, pm. 1906)*

The Silver King Saloon, left foreground, was part of this Main/Military Plaza block soon demolished for widening Commerce Street (running diagonally from lower left) and for a new Frost Bank. In the distance is the old double-towered courthouse. *(Nig Tengg, pm. 1907)*

A wider Commerce Street with the new Frost National Bank building in the rest of the block is seen from the opposite direction of the view at the top of page. *(n.p., ca. 1935)*

Commerce Street, then the city's premier business artery, is seen looking east from the northeast corner of Main Plaza. Left of center is the landmark Hertzberg Clock, later moved to the corner of Houston and St. Mary's streets. *(Sam Rosenthall, San Antonio, pm. 1911)*

A streetcar enters the northwest corner of Main Plaza past the corner block of shops in center around which was wrapped the 1971 Frost National Bank Building and parking garage. *(n.p., pm. 1912)*

For a moment in time San Fernando Cathedral was bordered by both the 1921 Frost Bank building and the original city hall, its turrets and clock tower removed in 1927 to accommodate a third story. *(n.p., ca. 1925)*

The transformed city hall shows at far left. In the right foreground, is a bandstand with public restrooms below. In the left foreground, a parking lot has appeared on the future site of San Fernando's 2003 Cathedral Centre. *(Weiner News Co., San Antonio, ca. 1940)*

San Fernando Cathedral.   SAN ANTONIO, Tex.

The apse of the original parish church of San Fernando,
built in 1738, shows in this view from the top of city hall
prior to its being hidden by an addition in the 1920s.
(Brown News Co., ca. 1910)

SAN FERNANDO CATHEDRAL RECTORY, SAN ANTONIO, TEXAS 958-30

A new rectory addition hid San Fernando's original apse, revealed again and restored when the addition was removed in 1971. *(Nic Tengg, San Antonio, ca. 1930)*

INT. OF SAN FERNANDO CATHEDRAL SAN ANTONIO, TEX.

A magnificent nave was completed in 1873 when new walls on three sides of San Fernando were built around the original walls, then taken down and removed through the front door. *(H. Budow, San Antonio, ca. 1910)*

Main Plaza and Bexar Co. Court House, San Antonio, Texas.

Bexar County's fourth courthouse, a Romanesque Revival landmark, was built on the south side of Main Plaza in 1892. It regained much of its original splendor in a restoration that began in 2002. The Nat Washer Building is at the left. *(Nic Tengg, San Antonio, ca. 1905)*

22—Mexican Water Cart, San Antonio, Texas.   SAUL WOLFSON D. G. CO.

This water vendor pauses at the rear of the courthouse, as he continued to do business the old way in a time when San Antonio's water system did not yet reach all residents of the city. *(Saul Wolfson Co., ca. 1900)*

Bexar County Court House. San Antonio, Texas.

Ed. Sachs, Pub. San Antonio, Tex.

A billboard advertising *Sweet Sixteen* at the Grand Opera House rises behind a Southern Pacific Depot-bound streetcar making a stop at the courthouse. *(Ed Sachs, San Antonio, pm. 1908)*

In this view, Main Avenue is yet to be cut through past the right of the courthouse. That would remove the old Elliott's Flats building, a printshop at this point on its ground floor. Parking space in the area, then as now, was a choice commodity. *(np., ca. 1925)*

Balconies overlooking Main Plaza came with rooms at Elliott's Flats—a good cigar was once a nickel—until the building was razed when Main Avenue was extended past the courthouse in 1929. *(n.p., ca. 1905)*

3. Alamo Plaza

By the time picture postcards gained popularity early in the twentieth century, Alamo Plaza was surrounded by many of the city's finest buildings—the best hotel, an opera house, the federal courthouse/post office, major office buildings and fine stores. Only shortly before, in 1876, cattle were corraled in the then-relatively deserted plaza for the first public demonstration of barbed wire.

The spot across a bend of the San Antonio River east of the main town had been chosen in 1724 as the third—and final—location of Mission San Antonio de Valero, which became known as the Alamo. The mission's permanent church was begun in 1744, but remained unfinished when the mission closed in 1793. The abandoned mission was fortified in 1836 by a band of Texas independence fighters, soon overwhelmed by Santa Anna's Mexican Army.

Decades later, a public plaza took shape around the approximate boundaries of the old mission plaza. The restored Alamo church facing the plaza retains its appeal as a ceremonial focal point and as one of the state's top tourist attractions.

The Alamo's frame-covered convento had become a jarring intrusion into the increasingly fashionable Alamo Plaza when this view was made from the roof of the old post office building, looking toward the turreted 1890 Federal Building. *(n.p., ca. 1905)*

Alamo Plaza, San Antonio Texas, on December 14th., 1898
The first snow in San Antonio, Texas, for many years.

57

Even the nearby San Antonio River froze when this snow dusted San Antonio in December 1898, slowing activity around usually-bustling Alamo Plaza to a near halt. *(n.p., ca. 1900)*

By the early 20th century, Alamo Plaza had exceeded Main and Military plazas as a commercial center. Carriages in right foreground await fares from guests at the Menger Hotel, off the view at right. *(H. Budow, San Antonio, pm. 1912)*

Cars were double-parking as Alamo Plaza's growth boomed with construction of the Medical Arts Building in the late 1920s. *(n.p., ca. 1930)*

Alamo Plaza, San Antonio, Texas.—25

To alleviate traffic pressures, Crockett Street was cut across Alamo Plaza in the foreground. The original bandstand was removed and replaced with one of rock and concrete, in center foreground. *(E. C. Kropp Co., Milwaukee, ca. 1935)*

In this view looking south from the Federal Building, at left foreground a crenelated frame exterior sheaths Hugo, Schmeltzer and Company's Alamo Building, its interior remains dating from the Alamo's Spanish mission days. *(n.p., pm. 1907)*

Some 40 years after the view at the top of the page, carriages and streetcars were gone, the Hugo, Schmeltzer building was reduced to a single-story shell and an apparently cast-iron fountain was replaced by a cenotaph honoring Alamo heroes. *(n.p., ca. 1950)*

Gates at the Alamo's parklike courtyard open to the
front of the old Alamo mission church, begun in 1744.
(n.p., ca. 1945)

The Alamo. Built in 1718. San Antonio, Tex.

At the turn of the century, a star of electric lights adorned the parapet of the old Alamo church, purchased from the Catholic Church by the State of Texas in 1883 and opened to visitors. *(George M. Bierce, San Antonio, ca. 1905)*

The Alamo (built 1718)
San Antonio Texas.

THE ALAMO. The Cradle of Texas liberty was built 1718 was taken by the Mexican Army under Santa Anna in 1836 in which battle 177 Texans were fighting against 6000 Mexicans.

The gate of a picket fence near the south wall of the Alamo church opened to an alley to the Gallagher home, on private land at the back. *(Charles Apelt, Comfort, Tex., ca. 1905)*

Never completed by Spanish missionaries, the Alamo church got a frame roof from the U.S. Army, which used it as as a supply depot. A vaulted concrete roof was installed in time for the Texas Centennial in 1936. *(George M. Bearce, San Antonio, ca. 1905)*

A floral Texas star was planted in an inner courtyard as the Alamo evolved into today's shrine honoring those who died in the Battle of the Alamo in 1836. *(Nic Tengg, San Antonio, ca. 1925)*

An automobile dealership was housed in the brick building beside the Alamo church until the adjacent land was purchased and latter-day buildings razed at the time of the 1936 Texas Centennial. *(Dahrooge Post Card Co., San Antonio, ca. 1910)*

A Victorian-era bandstand was a focal point of Alamo Plaza at the beginning of the 20th century. *(George M. Bearce, ca. 1905)*

San Antonio's ubiquitous candy merchants were also busy on Alamo Plaza in the early 20th century. *(Sam Rosenthall, San Antonio, ca. 1910)*

BAND STAND AND REST ROOM SHOWING THE ALAMO AND ALAMO PLAZA, SAN ANTONIO, TEX.

Alamo Plaza's new concrete and stone bandstand also addressed a growing demand for public restrooms in the city. *(S. Rabe, San Antonio, ca. 1925)*

San Antonio, the largest city in Texas from 1890 to 1930, prided itself in its open spaces downtown. *(Nic Tengg, San Antonio, ca. 1925)*

Palm trees, though endangered by occasional freezing weather, frame the turret of the city's 1890 Richardson Romanesque Federal Building and Post Office. *(n.p., ca. 1915)*

San Antonio's Federal Building and Post Office shared the block with the Arthur Hotel, left rear, and, hidden behind at the right, the first Elks Club Building. *(n.p., ca. 1930)*

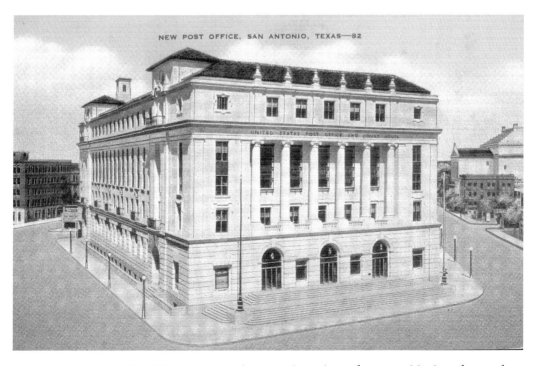

A new, larger Federal Building in a neoclassic style took up the entire block at the north end of Alamo Plaza when it was built in 1937. *(E. C. Kropp Co., Milwaukee, ca. 1940)*

Traditional outdoor food sellers so typical of San Antonio's earlier times seem out of place among the modern buildings of northern Alamo Plaza in a new century. *(Nic Tengg, San Antonio, pm. 1912)*

The five-story Maverick Bank Building, built in 1885 at the northwest corner of Alamo Plaza and Houston Street, is shown as an office building before its demolition for a Woolworth's outlet in 1919. *(S. H. Kress & Co., pm. 1916)*

In this view west from Alamo Plaza, low buildings at the right are about to be replaced by the stylish eight-story Gibbs Building. *(Adolph Selige Co., St. Louis, ca. 1905)*

Alamo Plaza and Houston Street were headed toward midcentury, but an edge of the turret of the yet-to-be-replaced Federal Building still shows at the far right. *(Weiner News Co., San Antonio, ca. 1935)*

Stylish Victorian facades adorned the west side of Alamo Plaza as the transition from horsedrawn to motorized vehicles was under way. The Plaza Theater's sign projects at far right. *(H. Budow, San Antonio, ca. 1915)*

Alamo Plaza's Plaza Theater, built for vaudeville performances, later added silent films to its schedule. *(Dahrooge Co., San Antonio., ca. 1915)*

Increasing traffic south from Alamo Plaza to Commerce Street caused Alamo Street to be widened in 1913, shearing off building facades on the right. *(Nic Tengg, San Antonio, ca. 1910)*

Respite from the hubub outside could be found at C. W. McCabe's Plaza Bar, across Blum Street from the Menger Hotel. *(Malzman & Rehfield, Oklahoma City, ca. 1915)*

The steeple of St. Joseph's Catholic Church on Commerce Street is a focal point of this view of Alamo Plaza to the southeast. *(n.p., ca. 1910)*

Draughon's Practical Business College draped its banner across its home in the Reuter Building, far right, in this view southwest from the Alamo. *(H. Budow, San Antonio, pm. 1916)*

Alamo Plaza. Reuter Building. Opera House. Wickes Building.
San Antonio, Texas.

23

Dominating the west central face of Alamo Plaza at the start of the 20th century were, from left, the Reuter Building, which survives and has been restored; the turetted Grand Opera House, built in 1886; and the Wickes Building. *(n.p., ca. 1900)*

MEXICAN CHILE STANDS, ALAMO PLAZA, SAN ANTONIO

Judging from the bunting on buildings and the festive striped tents at far right center, these outdoor food vendors could have been preparing for a Fiesta parade. *(n.p., ca. 1905)*

ALAMO PLAZA AND MENGER HOTEL, SAN ANTONIO, TEX.

Framing the southeastern corner of Alamo Plaza were the Menger Hotel, center, and, to its right, the pre-1890 post office building, then occupied by the New York Life Insurance Company. *(Walter L. Dalbey, Richmond, Ind., pm. 1908)*

Menger Hotel, San Antonio, Tex.

The Menger Hotel opened on the undeveloped Alamo Plaza in 1859. The wing at the left was added some three decades later. *(International Post Card Co., New York, pm. 1909)*

In a setting more peaceful than that of hotels on the noisy Main and Military plazas, the Menger Hotel became a prestigious address for visitors. *(S. H. Kress & Co., ca. 1910)*

Present-day diners at the Menger Hotel can recognize features of its originial dining room. *(H. Budow, San Antonio, ca. 1910)*

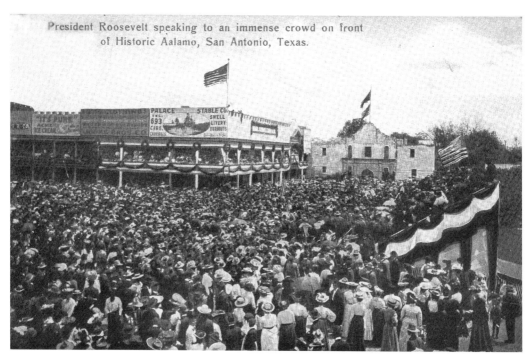

Ever since the valiant but ill-fated stand of its defenders in 1836, Alamo Plaza has retained ceremonial significance. Here President Theodore Roosevelt addresses a crowd from a since-removed balcony in 1905. *(Grombach-Faisans Co., New Orleans, 1905)*

Since 1891, Alamo Plaza has been the focal point of the Battle of Flowers parade marking the Texans' victory at San Jacinto in 1836, shortly after the fall of the Alamo. *(n.p., ca. 1905)*

4. Travis Park

While Military, Main and Alamo plazas have roots in Spanish times and reflect the commercial evolution of San Antonio, Travis Park has kept its calmer, residential aura, even though its elegant homes are now gone.

Well-shaded Travis Park has the most Southern feeling of San Antonio's parks and plazas. Dominated by the Confederate soldiers' memorial dedicated in 1900 by the local chapter of the United Daughters of the Confederacy, Travis Park is faced by two churches—Episcopal and Methodist—of the four houses of worship once on its borders. Along the south side remains the doyenne of the San Antonio's twentieth century hotels, the St. Anthony.

Earlier the park was the orchard of pioneers Samuel A. and Mary Maverick, who donated it. Named for Alamo commander William Barret Travis, it was a bivouac site for Confederate Army recruits during the Civil War, and once had its own bandstand and horsehoe-pitching courts. In the 1950s Travis Park survived an attempt to dig it up for an 1,100-car underground parking garage.

Travis Park & Confederate Monument. San Antonio, Texas

Some of the homes that once lined Travis Park are visible in this view of the monument to Confederate soldiers who died in the Civil War. *(n.p., ca. 1905)*

The bandstand placed in Travis Park in 1883 is near the center of this view, with Travis Park Methodist Church at far left. The bandstand was removed in 1936. *(International Post Card Co., New York, ca. 1910)*

Tallest of these vanished structures west of Travis Park was the Travis Club, later the Elks' Club. The 1912 building was dynamited in 1978 to make way for a parking lot. Its image is preserved on boxes of San Antonio-made Travis Club Cigars. *(n.p., ca. 1910)*

The domed Temple Beth-El is in the foreground of this skyline view of eastern downtown San Antonio, apparently seen looking from the roof of St. Mark's Episcopal Church. *(Paul Ebers, San Antonio, ca. 1910)*

THE OLD CANNON THAT WAS USED IN 1836, NOW IN TRAVIS PARK, SAN ANTONIO, TEXAS.

Despite the assertion that this cannon, one of two now near the Confederate monument, was used in the Battle of the Alamo, it more likely dates from the Civil War. *(Acmegraph Co., Chicago, ca. 1910)*

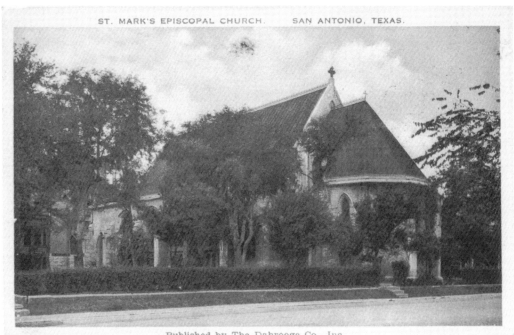

The Gothic Revival St. Mark's Episcopal Church was begun in 1859, though not completed until 1875. Its designer was Richard Upjohn, also architect of Trinity Church at the head of New York City's Wall Street. *(Dahrooge Co., San Antonio, ca. 1915)*

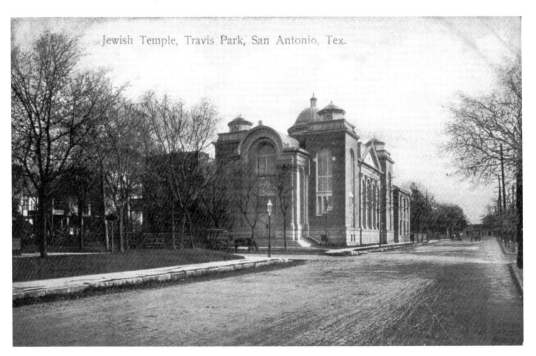

Jewish Temple, Travis Park, San Antonio, Tex.

Temple Beth-El was built at the southeast corner of Travis Park in 1903, on the site of an earlier temple building. It was razed after the congregation moved to Belknap Place some two decades later. *(International Post Card Co., New York, ca. 1910)*

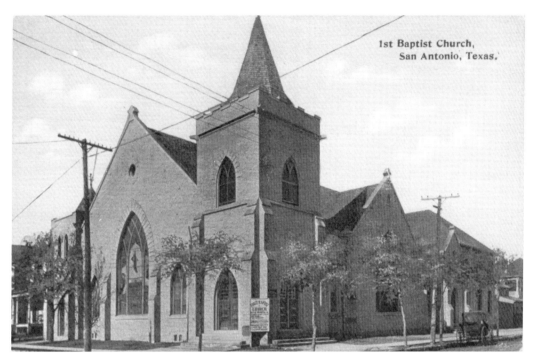

First Baptist Church built this home across Travis Street from Temple Beth-El in 1871, and moved to its present complex on McCullough Avenue before World War II. *(Dahrooge Co., ca. 1910*

Travis Park Methodist Church built this structure at the southwest corner of Travis Park in 1883, and has expanded at the same location. *(International Post Card Co., New York, ca. 1910)*

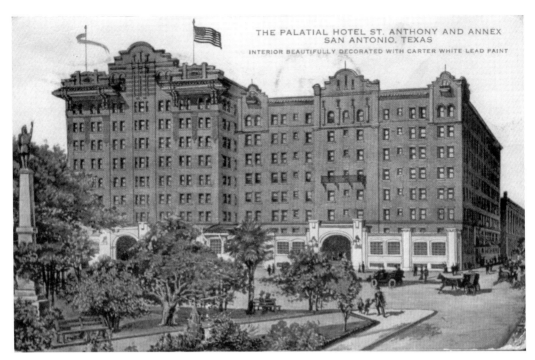

THE PALATIAL HOTEL ST. ANTHONY AND ANNEX
SAN ANTONIO. TEXAS

INTERIOR BEAUTIFULLY DECORATED WITH CARTER WHITE LEAD PAINT

The first section of the St. Anthony Hotel, left, was built facing Travis Park in 1910 in an Alamo/Mission Revival style. It was soon followed by a new wing. With a pioneering air conditioning system, it quickly became San Antonio's premier hotel. *(n.p., pm. 1911)*

Addition of a tenth floor came with a renovation to unify the St. Anthony's facade and cement the claim that it was "the world's largest completely and continuously air conditioned hotel." *(Curt Teich Co., Chicago, pm. 1941)*

5. River Walk

San Antonio's River Walk has evolved into one of the world's most renowned linear parks. Although much of the river's flow through downtown is now recycled with the aid of a subterranean flood control tunnel, and is carefully managed in a computer operations center downstream, to outward appearances the picturesque river downtown remains primarily a creation of nature.

These postcard images document the River Walk's evolution from the days when residents picked their way along its banks carefully—if they could get through the underbrush at all. Landscaping that began in 1904 was followed ten years later by a channeled park, transformed in 1939–41 by the Works Progress Administration using the design of architect Robert H. H. Hugman.

Hugman's two original bridges— arched to accommodate gondoliers in what was envisioned as the "Venice of America"—have been replicated several times in various forms, and numerous other changes have been made, but today's River Walk remains true to to the original plan.

SAN ANTONIO   River from Mill Bridge.

Looking west to the courthouse, the future site of this portion of the River Walk is little more than an occasional path. The carriages are in the water so their wooden wheels can expand more tightly within the metal rims. *(Rafael Tuck & Sons, London, ca. 1905)*

The shaded river winding through a busy downtown was a great attraction for visitors in the 19th and early 20th centuries. *(Acmegraph Co., Chicago, ca. 1905)*

Arrival of the railroad in the 1870s made it easier for the city to get shipments from the East of cast iron bridges to cross the narrow river. *(S. H. Kress & Co., ca. 1905)*

Looking from the Crockett Street bridge west to Commerce Street, what is now one of the busiest sections of the River Walk was then overgrown and deserted. *(n.p., ca. 1905)*

One of the earliest sections of the river to have its brush clipped, trees trimmed and pathways used is this one below Crockett Street as seen from the St. Mary's Street bridge, with the future site of La Mansion del Rio Hotel at the left. *(Joske Bros., San Antonio, ca. 1905)*

Native plants thrived then as now on the banks of the San Antonio River, as seen in this view looking through the southern Navarro Street bridge to the courthouse and San Fernando Cathedral. *(Nic Tengg, San Antonio, pm. 1910)*

The widest part of the river, near the end of the southern leg of the Great Bend, required a double-span bridge for Navarro Street. *(Nic Tengg, San Antonio, ca. 1910)*

A dam across the river held back water to power the 1845 Nat Lewis Mill, which gave the Navarro Street bridge the designation Mill Bridge. *(Nic Tengg, San Antonio, ca. 1905)*

Two major floods in 1913 and a worse one in 1921 led to construction of a dam across a watershed upstream and a straight flood channel downtown, so floodgates could protect the Great Bend from such sights as this and allow safe development. *(n.p., pm. 1914)*

SAN ANTONIO RIVER. SAN ANTONIO. TEXAS.

Published by The Dahrooge Co., Inc.

In 1914 the city landscaped the downtown riverbanks
and built concrete walls, as in this section of the northern
leg of the Great Bend below the St. Mary's Street bridge.
(Dahrooge Co., San Antonio, ca. 1920)

The Hyatt Regency Hotel now stands at the left of this section of the river's Great Bend looking toward the Crockett Street bridge. *(Dahrooge Co., San Antonio, ca. 1925)*

This section of the river from Crockett Street toward the Commerce Street bridge is in marked contrast to the earlier view at the top of page 45. *(Weiner News, San Antonio, ca. 1935)*

Ravaged by the 1921 flood, the Mill Bridge over Navarro Street was replaced by this arched concrete span. The courthouse is in the distance. *(H. L. Summerville, San Antonio, ca. 1925)*

SAN ANTONIO, TEXAS

The 1929 skyscraper now known as the Tower Life Building is shown in this favorite view from the landscaped riverbanks. *(Weiner News Co., San Antonio, ca. 1935)*

5—*Plaza Hotel—Fiesta Time, San Antonio, Texas*

The Plaza Hotel's Jack White in 1936 revived the tradition of Fiesta river parades. *(Weiner News Co., San Antonio, ca. 1936)*

The Plaza Hotel-backed river beautification project, undertaken by the Works Progress Administration in 1939–41, was intended to make San Antonio no less than the "Venice of America." *(E. C. Kropp Co., Milwaukee, ca. 1940)*

The completed San Antonio River beautification project, designed by architect Robert H. H. Hugman, transformed the banks of the river. *(Weiner News Co, San Antonio, ca. 1945)*

A main feature of the new San Antonio River Walk was an outdoor theater with an arched entry from the La Villita area of newly-restored homes above the river. *(n.p., ca. 1945)*

A bridge across the San Antonio River provided access from the sloped seating area on the left to the outdoor stage on the right. *(Weiner News Co., San Antonio, ca. 1945)*

Along the San Antonio River, Venice of America.
San Antonio, Texas   35

Photo by Harvey Patteson

Flagstones with gaps so water can flow into the river
from a cascade force pedestrians to pay attention to their
surroundings. *(San Antonio Card Co., ca. 1945)*

In this view toward the Commerce Street bridge, a recently-constructed stairway rises to street level to the left of the river-level office then occupied by River Walk architect Robert Hugman. *(n.p., ca. 1945)*

The first river-level business along the Great Bend was Casa Rio, a restaurant established in 1946 that is still in business. *(C. F. Searls & Son, San Antonio, ca. 1950)*

6. San Pedro Park

San Antonio began near San Pedro Springs, source of a ten-mile creek that flows into the San Antonio River. In 1718 this was the first site of San Antonio's military presidio and of the mission that, in its third location, achieved fame as the Alamo. The area was reserved for public use by the king of Spain in 1729. San Antonio's first military training center was set up here during the Mexican War.

Formally made a city park in 1852, the scenic spot became a favorite retreat from town. Citizens arrived in greater numbers beginning in 1878, when San Pedro Park became the terminus of the new mule-drawn streetcar line that began at Alamo Plaza, two miles to the southeast. Activities ranged from boating on the lake to viewing caged animals in a privately-run zoo.

San Pedro Park was at its scenic peak when these postcard images appeared. But the water table was dropping, and plans to replace dwindling spring waters by pumping did not survive the Depression. Thanks to periodic rebeautification efforts, San Pedro Park remains green, if no longer lush.

The city's premier park at the start of the 20th century was San Pedro Park, the "Garden Spot of San Antonio." *(Souvenir Post Card Co., New York, ca. 1905)*

SAN ANTONIO SPRINGS—SAN ANTONIO, TEXAS.

The springs in San Pedro Park kept this lake full, until increased use of artesian wells at the start of the 20th century brought a falling water table, causing the springs to flow intermittently. *(Missouri, Kansas & Texas Ry. Co., ca. 1905)*

San Pedro Springs. San Antonio, Texas.

Shaded, rock-lined banks surrounded San Pedro Park's lake. *(Adolph Selige Pub. Co., St. Louis, ca. 1905)*

"Homes" for water birds were once a feature of San Pedro Park's lake. *(Paul Ebers, San Antonio, pm. 1910)*

In 18th and 19th century San Antonio, springs that filled this lake also supplied an acequia, one of the irrigation ditches comprising the city's first water system. *(George M. Bearce, San Antonio, ca. 1910)*

19—"Terrace," San Pedro Springs, San Antonio, Texas.   SAUL WOLFSON D G CO.

Rock-walled terraces above the San Pedro springs foreshadowed the later rockwork of the San Antonio River Walk. *(Saul Wolfson Co., ca. 1900)*

San Pedro Park. San Antonio, Texas.

Landscaped walks stretched throughout the 40-acre San Pedro Park. *(Adolph Selige Pub. Co., St. Louis, ca. 1905)*

Children had their own pool, with a shallow water level and a bridge. *(Acmegraph Co., Chicago, ca. 1910)*

The lake at San Pedro Springs was replaced by this city swimming pool. *(Nic Tengg, San Antonio, pm. 1931)*

When origins of a landmark are obscure, legends rush in to fill the vacuum. This structure of old but unknown provenance was passed off variously as Santa Anna's home . . . *(S. H. Kress & Co., pm. 1915)*

OLD ARSENAL POWDER HOUSE AT SAN PEDRO PARK, SAN ANTONIO, TEX.

. . . as an "old arsenal powder house" . . . *(Dahrooge Co., San Antonio, ca. 1915)*

9—Old Mexican Fort, San Pedro Springs, San Antonio, Texas.   SAUL WOLFSON D. G CO.

. . . as an "old Mexican fort" . . . *(Saul Wolfson Co., ca. 1900)*

Scene In San Pedro Park, Showing Old Mexican Dwelling, San Antonio, Texas.

"The Winter Playground of America."

. . . and simply as an "old Mexican dwelling." Most probably a blockhouse for protection against Indian raids, it was restored in 2002. *(Hewitt News Service, SanAntonio, ca. 1925)*

SAN ANTONIO ACADEMY, SAN ANTONIO, TEX.

Two-year-old San Antonio Academy, a boys' military school, moved in 1888 to face the western edge of San Pedro Park, and stayed until it moved 10 blocks away in 1967. *(n.p., ca. 1915)*

Named to capitalize on the new availability and popularity of electricity, Electric Park for a decade offered rides and amusements facing the southern edge of San Pedro Park. *(George M. Bearce, San Antonio, pm. 1910)*

7. Brackenridge Park

Near the headwaters of the San Antonio River and once valued for its role in the city's first municipal water system, Brackenridge Park was created in 1899 by mogul George Brackenridge's donation of 199 acres of riverside land. Five times the size of San Pedro Park, a mile and a half to the southwest, Brackenridge Park gradually took over as the city's main recreation center.

When the donor's ban on consumption of alcoholic beverages inspired the nickname "Prohibition Park," Emma Koehler, widow of brewer Otto Koehler, donated 11 adjacent acres, where consumption of beer was specifically permitted.

Cliffs left by a quarry on the northern edge lent a dramatic setting for the San Antonio Zoo. Nearby, a pit beside an abandoned cement plant was transformed into a sunken garden. Bathhouses for swimming and pavilions for picnicking rose beside the river, and picturesque drives were cut through dense woods. A golf course at the park's southern end and two museums facing Broadway on the eastern boundary help maintain the now-320-acre park's significance to the city.

In a region known for hot summers and semi-arid hinterlands, the shaded riverside lushness of Brackenridge quickly became a favorite retreat for San Antonians. *(n.p., ca. 1910)*

Grazing in a fenced area of what is now the Brackenridge Park Golf Course are buffalo brought by George Brackenridge from Yellowstone National Park. *(Ebers-White, San Antonio, ca. 1910)*

Along with ten buffalo, Brackenridge brought six elk from Yellowstone Park to graze in the new parkland. *(Nic Tengg, San Antonio, ca. 1910)*

Elk in San Antonio River, at Brackenridge Park, San Antonio, Tex.

The San Antonio River provided a cool refuge for these elk on a summer day. *(George M. Bearce, San Antonio, ca. 1910)*

DEER AT BRACKENRIDGE PARK   Published by Joske Bros. Co., San Antonio, Tex.

Deer brought in to join the buffalo and elk were moved to the northern part of the park in 1914 as the beginning of the San Antonio Zoo. *(Joske Bros., San Antonio, ca. 1910)*

Spanish moss hanging from trees added a dramatic note to densely wooded portions of the park. *(George M. Bearce, San Antonio, ca. 1910)*

Flowering trees were planted along roadways in open areas of Brackenridge Park. *(Dahrooge Co., San Antonio, ca. 1910)*

Automobiles soon made their appearance. *(Nic Tengg, San Antonio, ca. 1910)*

The bust of Park Commissioner Ludwig Mahncke in the inset was placed in adjacent Mahncke Park, a strip of land once used for pipes carrying water eastward up to the city reservoir on the site of the present-day Botanical Garden. *(Paul Ebers, San Antonio, pm. 1911)*

A stone bridge over the San Antonio River was a feature of the park named in 1901 on the site of Ilka Nursery, owned by Helen "Ilka" Madarasz, a Hungarian immigrant whose name no one else seemed able to spell. *(Paul Ebers, San Antonio, ca. 1910)*

The 3.5-acre Madarasz Park, on the site of a Confederate tannery, was purchased in 1883 from George Brackenridge by Helen Madarasz and sold by her heirs to Otto Koehler. *(F. C. Vietus, pm. 1907)*

What may be remains of the Madarasz Park bridge appear above after the park was included in the 11 acres donated by the widow of brewer Otto Koehler as Koehler Park, adjoining the zoo. *(Hewitt News Service, San Antonio, ca. 1920)*

Picnics in Edwardian times were formal affairs. *(H. Budow, San Antonio, ca. 1910)*

A faux wooden entrance by concrete artisan Dionicio Rodriguez marks the entrance to the Japanese Sunken Gardens' Tea Garden. The name was changed to Chinese Gardens with the advent of World War II, but restored to the original name in 1983. *(n.p., ca. 1945)*

The Sunken Gardens were created in the abandoned quarry of the earliest Portland cement company west of the Mississippi, begun in 1880 and abandoned in 1908. The gardens were created in 1917 under Parks Commissioner Ray Lambert. *(n.p., ca. 1940)*

Stone paths and ornamental rockwork were built with the aid of prisoners' labor. A former kiln's smokestack shows at above right center. *(Zark Studio, Sulphur, Okla., ca. 1920)*

A floral Texas star was created on the future site of the Sunken Garden Theater. This view is toward Brackenridge Park's onetime polo grounds, now a golf driving range. *(C. E. Kropp Co., Milwaukee, ca. 1925)*

The Sunken Garden Theater opened in the summer of 1930. Its facilities were completed in 1937 by the Works Progress Administration, with the aid of Texas Centennial funding. *(San Antonio Card Co., ca. 1940)*

Brackenridge Park's 18-hole golf course in 1923 got this new clubhouse, designed by architect Ralph Cameron to replace the two-story, galleried Jockey Club built for the racetrack once near the site. *(n.p., ca. 1925)*

LAMBERT'S BEACH, BRACKENRIDGE PARK, SAN ANTONIO, TEX.

Lambert's Beach was created with stone and concrete on a bend of the San Antonio River in northern Brackenridge Park in 1917 and named in honor of energetic Park Commissioner Ray Lambert. It closed in 1950. *(Dahrooge Co., San Antonio, pm. 1917)*

BATH HOUSE, BATHING BEACH, BRACKENRIDGE PARK. SAN ANTONIO, TEXAS.

Published by The Dahrooge Co., Inc.

A pumping station built by the San Antonio Water Works Company in 1877 was converted to a bathhouse for Lambert's Beach. *(Dahrooge Co., San Antonio, ca. 1920)*

WITTE MEMORIAL MUSEUM
SAN ANTONIO, TEXAS

The Witte Memorial Museum opened in 1926 in this Spanish Colonial Revival style building, designed by Robert M. Ayres. It faces Broadway on the northeastern edge of Brackenridge Park. *(San Antonio Card Co., ca. 1940)*

Texas Pioneers, Trail Drivers and Rangers Memorial Building
Brackenridge Park   San Antonio, Texas

This museum, now known as Pioneer Hall, was completed north of the Witte in 1937. It also serves as headquarters for the Texas Trail Drivers Association, memorializing those who drove cattle through Texas in the late 19th century. *(n.p., ca. 1945)*

As a Depression-era fundraising effort, the Witte Museum in 1932 opened the nearby Reptile Research Garden, renamed Alligator Garden when snakes were replaced with alligators in 1950. It was closed in 1975. *(Weiner News Agency, San Antonio, ca. 1955)*

While the curious and hungry look on from above, snakes are fried in a pit of the Reptile Gardens as an ongoing Depression-era fundraising effort. The chef is identified as Tex Sullivan, his assistant as A. B. Stokes. *(n.p., ca 1935)*

Limestone cliffs cut during the area's time as a quarry provide the setting for what were then drive-up exhibits of African animals. *(Hewitt News Service, San Antonio, ca. 1925)*

Broad trenches in the foreground have since kept lions and tigers a safe distance from spectators, removing the need for steel cages. *(n.p., ca. 1925)*

Sea lions sunning themselves on a rock entertained this group of 1920s visitors to Brackenridge Park's zoo. *(n.p., ca. 1925)*

The home of the camel named Lady Mae was maintained in the zoo by the Alzafar Temple Shrine. *(n.p., ca. 1925)*

"The seals and elephants put on a good act," the sender of this card wrote home on the back. "One of the bears posed for us to take his picture, but we didn't have a camera." *(San Antonio Card Co., pm. 1943)*

The Brackenridge Park Zoo's closeness to the headwaters of the San Antonio River is a boon to these hippos. *(Nic Tengg, San Antonio, ca. 1930)*

The limestone outcroppings and trees of Monkey Island provided a playground for monkeys until recent times. *(E. C. Kropp Co., Milwaukee, ca. 1935)*

Caves cut into limestone cliffs provide a natural shelter for bears and other animals in neighboring exhibit areas. *(E. C. Kropp Co., Milwaukee, ca. 1935)*

Chimpanzees, San Antonio Zoo, San Antonio, Texas

"These apes are born mimics, they delight in imitating the actions of human beings," reads the caption on the back of this postcard. *(San Antonio Post Card Co., ca. 1940)*

8. Other Plazas and Parks

As San Antonio grew during the nineteenth century, the Spanish tradition of plazas continued through residential parks in new neighborhoods. Some, like Madison Park, retain a residential flavor, though bisected by later thoroughfares. Others, like Maverick Park, have lost that sense altogether. More distant parks like Woodlawn Lake still keep a feeling of spaciousness in a suburban setting.

A few parks have disappeared, like Paschal Square in front of the 1900 Market House. In that case, nearby Milam Park took up the slack, and during the nuclear scare of the 1950s survived a proposal that it become the site of an underground bomb shelter serviced by the staff of nearby Santa Rosa Hospital.

The 1950s was a particularly perilous time for downtown parks, as businesses targeted several—Main Plaza, Alamo Plaza, Travis Park and Madison Square, among others—as sites for building projects, or for above- or below-ground parking facilities to compete with sprawling new suburban malls. But conservationists flew to the barricades, and such plans were ultimately defeated.

As San Antonio grew outward, five-acre Madison Square, its earliest section set aside in 1847, was surrounded by stately turn-of-the-twentieth-century homes. (*Dahrooge Co., San Antonio, ca. 1910*)

Milam Park, created in 1883 on the site of a public cemetery, is in the center of this view looking northwest from the old city hall cupola. *(Nic Tengg, San Antonio, ca. 1905)*

Milam Park was named for Ben Milam, killed in 1835 after leading a successful attack on a Mexican army occupying the town. Most graves on the site were removed, but Milam's was retained in the center of the park. *(Nic Tengg, San Antonio, pm. 1914)*

Milam Square (Santa Rosa Hospital in background). San Antonio, Texas.

Dominating the north side of Milam Park is Santa Rosa Hospital, the city's first, established in 1869 by the newly-arrived Sisters of Charity of the Incarnate Word. *(Adolph Selige Co., St. Louis, ca. 1905)*

New wings have since been added to earlier buildings in the course of Santa Rosa Hospital's ongoing growth. *(n.p., ca. 1945)*

San Antonio's third public market opened just south of Milam Park in 1900, its main entrance facing Paschal Square and its fountain. A convention hall on the second floor had a seating capacity advertised as 4,000. *(George M. Bearce, San Antonio, ca. 1910)*

The view east from the Market House—razed in 1938—included City Hall and the courthouse on the skyline and the F. A. Chapa Drug Store, right of center. In 1923, Paschal Square was covered by an annex to the market. *(Nic Tengg, San Antonio, pm. 1912)*

A PRETTY SCENE IN MAVERICK PARK, SAN ANTONIO, TEXAS.

Three-acre Maverick Park was donated in 1881 by Samuel Maverick Jr. Named Milam Park for its first two years, the park survived an attempt in 1929 to bisect it with a street linking Broadway and North Alamo Street. *(S. H. Kress & Co., ca. 1910)*

GARDEN ACADEMY SAN ANTONIO, TEX.

The home of Maverick Park donor Samuel Maverick Jr., at the southwest corner of Broadway and Tenth Street facing the park, became a military academy run by the Rev. Alfred W. S. Garden. *(Bobbe Litho Co., New York, ca. 1910)*

Romana Plaza, its bisected triangle since rejoined, was created in 1914 to anchor the head of a widened Soledad Street. Shown are the new Central Christian Church and Baptist Hospital. At upper right is part of Madison Square. *(Motion Film Service, San Antonio, ca. 1960)*

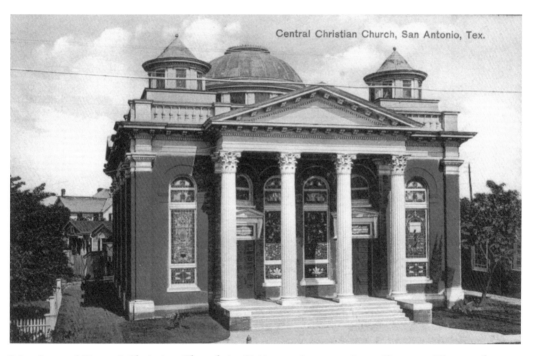

Members of Central Christian Church in 1941 voted to remain on Romana Plaza rather than move to a suburban location, and to replace their old church with the larger structure shown in the view at the top of the page. *(S. H. Kress & Co., ca. 1910)*

Romana Plaza was created just west of Physicians' and Surgeons' Hospital, a private institution opened in 1902 by a group of doctors and now the site of Baptist Hospital. *(Paul Ebers, San Antonio, pm. 1911)*

A dam developers built on Alazan Creek in the late 19th century created West End Lake. In 1918 the lake and adjacent land were donated and evolved into today's 62-acre Woodlawn Lake Park. *(International Post Card Co., New York, ca. 1905)*

While some military academies were close to regular parks that could double as drill grounds, Peacock's proximity to West End Lake gave it the promotional edge of swimming and boating activies. *(San Antonio Printing Co., ca. 1905)*

The West End/Woodlawn Lake campus occupied by Peacock Military Academy from its founding in 1894 to its closing in 1973 is now the Salvation Army's Peacock Center. *(n.p., ca. 1945)*

Military order was part of the regimen of J. W. Coltrane's Lakeside Classical Institute, at the southern shore of West End Lake. The building later housed the girls' Thomas School. *(Sam Rosenthall, San Antonio, ca. 1910)*

The city swimming pool at the eastern tip of Woodlawn Lake Park was originally surrounded by lights. *(n.p., ca. 1925)*

From 1888 to 1910, the San Antonio International Fair was held some two miles south of downtown in part of Riverside Park, where Theodore Roosevelt trained his Rough Riders in 1898. In 1920 a new park nearby was named Roosevelt in his honor. *(n.p., ca. 1905)*

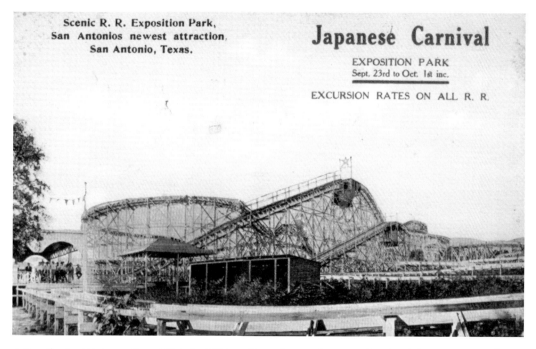

After the last International Fair in 1910, railroads sought to maintain ticket revenues from fairgoers throughout the state by promoting the short-lived Exposition Park, which opened on the site in 1911. *(H. Budow, San Antonio, ca. 1911)*

Index